Also by Floyd Collins

Scarecrow

The Wedding Guest

Forecast

Seamus Heaney: The Crisis of Identity

What Harvest: Poems on the Siege and Battle of the Alamo

The Living Artifact

MY BACK PAGES

The Teresa Poems

Floyd Collins

STEPHEN F. AUSTIN STATE UNIVERSITY PRESS

Production Manager: Kimberly Verhines

Book Design: Mallory LeCroy

IBSN: 978-1-62288-920-4

For more information: Stephen F. Austin State University Press

P.O. Box 13007 SFA Station

Nacogdoches, Texas 75962

sfapress@sfasu.edu

www.sfasu.edu/sfapress

936-468-1078

Distributed by Texas A&M University Press Consortium

www.tamupress.com

ACKNOWLEDGMENTS

Grateful acknowledgment is extended to the following journals, in
which these poems first appeared, some in slightly different versions:

The Arkansas Review: "Sleeping Over on Highway 78" "August 18, 1973"
"The Watch" "The Ghostly Heart" "Sound Wisdom" "The Machinery
of Night" "The Letter" "December, 1978"

The Georgia Review: "The Years Between" "The Waking Reverie"

The Gettysburg Review: "The Visitation" "Backward Glances"

Literary Matters: "Narcissus to the Muse" "Another Realm of Discourse"
"Elusive Couplings"

The Sewanee Review: "Expiation" "Farewell"

The Xavier Review: "Nights on the Delta"

for Teresa Lee Shuler

CONTENTS

Expiation   1

Farewell   5

The Visitation   6

Sleeping Over on Highway 78   7

August 18, 1973   8

The Years Between   10

The Waking Reverie   12

The Watch   13

The Ghostly Heart   15

Sound Wisdom   17

The Machinery of Night   19

The Letter   21

Backward Glances   23

December, 1978   26

Narcissus to the Muse   30

Two Parables   35

Nighthawks   37

Another Realm of Discourse   40

Self-Fashioning   42

Wavelengths   46

Late Chronicles   49

Dual Allegories   52

A Lapsed Paean   54

Potent Libations   57

Elusive Couplings   59

The Interlude   62

The Outcome   64

Nights on the Delta   67

The Full Reckoning   70

Author's Note   73

About the Author   75

EXPIATION

for Teresa Shuler

Still in our teens we walked the back paths
Of Overton Park, looking for a place,
The cider-tart odor of crab apples
Underfoot in the time of falling leaves.
I am haunted a half-century later by the lovely
Apparition of her face, the numinous
Ever-recurring almost nightly visitation
That frequents my troubled sleep, defying
All wakeful attempts to exorcise the memories
Of what receded so long ago. It remains,
That brief season that transpired in another age,
And years pass, deepening with time the fallen
Leaves of red and gold along lost ways that yet beguile.

MY BACK PAGES

FAREWELL

She died in the days before the autumn equinox,
Twenty-five years after our short liaison
Of adolescent bravura and stealth played out
Along wooded trails. Caught up in the masque
And pageant of the turning season, cool mornings
We uttered endearments a bit too clipped
For the particle vapor that issued from our lungs,
Frost dispersing above the tree line pyrotechnic
With color. Now she lies beneath the cold sod
Of Murray, Kentucky, in a coffin once shining
And upholstered like a new roadster. Pallbearers
Filed past the casket at graveside, each placing
On its lid a boutonnière blue as a robin's egg.
Oblivious to that untimely aneurysm, the ripe berry
Of blood that burst in her brain, I slumbered as the stars
Of the Milky Way wandered the disheveled clouds.
Too many years since our parting had intervened;
Another man's ring encircles her desiccated finger,
And she, too, sleeps on a little past the dream.

THE VISITATION

The night she died without my knowledge
Was a cool evening in mid-September;
Frost had not yet turned the cricket's heart
To silver. But what vexed sleep was the owl,
The grey-tufted harbinger who refused
To shuffle its feathers once and slumber
The whole night through upon its perch
In the black oak beyond the creek. When
I was finally able to pillow my head
In oblivion, she stood before me
As in life: her short, Gypsy shag
Yellow as a hayrick, the jade ring
I once gave her now worn like a trinket
About her neck. Her silence was eloquent
As any speech: it spoke of bitter loss,
And an infinite yearning for peace at our touch.

SLEEPING OVER ON HIGHWAY 78

for Richard Wooten

Thirty miles to the small town of Red Banks,
The phosphor-lit dial of your Opel Kadett's
Dashboard clock ticking out ten after ten,
A light rain intermittently stippling
The windshield with petti-tricolor drops
Smudged the next instant by the wipers'
Metronomic sway and rock, our
Antenna homing on Brenton Wood's
"Gimme Little Sign"; stars wandering
In a cirrus mist, we listen for the cricket
Scrabble in live bait shops, gold neon Jax
Blinking in the windows of darkened roadhouses
All along kudzu-hung Old Highway 78.

You brake hard, Rick, on the slow grade below
The trailer of red corrugated tin; the little
Dome-light tricks on when both doors
Swing wide, and we can hear the chert
Cracking under our boot-heels striding up
The wet gravel drive. Your mother, already
In her housecoat, rises from a wicker-backed
Kitchen chair, fetching out of the Frigidaire
Frosted glass goblets brimming apple cider.
Before heading for the paneled bedroom
We spin a Jr. Walker side, then turn in,
Each dreaming about her blue eyes,
Autumn rain pelting us to who-knows-where.

AUGUST 18, 1973

It is an August night in the Graceland suburb
Of this Delta metropolis, the blue leaves
Of trees heavy with dew as heat-stung
Cicadas, their wings thin as onion skin,
Send a somnolent chirr heavenward long
After the sun's orange quench to the west,
Where smoking bridge lamps vault
The mile-wide Mississippi into Arkansas.
Walking at midnight past the stadium
I remember the smell of sweat-stained leather,
Every steaming huddle as we drove
Toward the county championship that fall,
Our cleats clogged with sodden turf,
Every bone-jarring tackle beneath
Those Friday evening lambent beams
Bitten deep into my plastic mouthpiece.
No time then to gaze at you,
In your pleated cheerleader's skirt, kelly-green,
Your smooth skin burned brown
From indolent mornings spent poolside,
Short blonde shag cut shielded
From the icy glaze woven into a sun hat.
Now, three years later, I'm brought up short
In my reveries come far and hours too late
To the smoky globes and snuffed wicks
Of a dozen hurricane lanterns lining your drive.
The darkened panes of your two-story house
Proclaim the inhabitants now abed, each
Sunk in post-nuptial slumber, the shot glasses

Kindled with brandy now empty on a sideboard.
I recall also the vows we made
In that birch grove of gold autumn leaves,
Only the owl with its mane of winter lightning
To witness, as now the bride and her groom
Depart into mist where only the dreamer can follow.

THE YEARS BETWEEN

I watch the watery pitch of a black vinyl
33 r.p.m. graduate in ripples from the center
Like an oak's heartwood, diamond tip
Needle threading the eddying current where

The Beatles' side B medley on *Abbey Road*
Choirs of loads to be borne into a future
As yet unforeseen but portending solitude
If not dolor, nights spent in dim precincts

Of the lost and dissolute. I desired dominion
Over the page, the apt phrase, a lyric mastery
That accuses. Instead, you chose nurturing
The ill and ill-disposed, tapping with your IV

The likeliest vein, carrying the red vial before
You obliviously like a candle in a sleepwalker's
Dream. Diastole and systole, you took pulses
In fingers both tapered and cool while I sought

The lineaments of gratified desire in a heart
More figurative than literal. Did you recall
As I do, how in fall 1970, there were mornings
We would meet in a snug café over cinnamon

Rolls and coffee or sip frosted mugs of pale
Lager on leaf-strewn afternoons? Under age
For such libations, we were never carded. I
Still conjure the shared embraces too few

And far between. Mid-December we embarked
On paths no longer coincident; you graduated
From the Tennessee Medical College in 1974,
And I published the title poem of my first book

In *Epoch* at Cornell University the next year.
Reading your obituary in the *Paducah Sun's*
Black columns in September 1995 was like
Stepping on a long thorn: it ripped the breath

Clean out of me. Your age was listed as 42,
But in fact you were a year younger,
Although the surviving husband, the three
Children bereft of a mother rang dead true

As the knell of the First Christian Church
In Murray, Kentucky. A boy from the Delta,
I've grown old, a half-century of autumn leaves
Fallen between us like beaten gold, Teresa.

THE WAKING REVERIE

I stood on my back porch in the evening,
Alone. Like needlepoint, a few stars
Punched through the low-hanging clouds
And I listened to those big Canadian geese

Winging south, their long necks bent
To the migratory curve. I imagined you
Drifting beneath a satin counterpane,
How the brush before your darkened mirror

Crackled with enough static to lift this page
From your table of carved rosewood. In dreams
I walk those upstairs corridors twice fortunate,
Hoping to free your essence sealed in a bottle

Frosted green as absinthe. All poets partake
Of the harsh joy that attends solitude, but I
Conjure only you, reaching as I do for a ripe
Nectarine in my pocket, letting the juice trickle

Down my chin, the fruit not quite out of season
In this Delta suburb. In September, crickets
Still light up at moonrise, the toad's throat pulses
At the base of cracked masonry. But tonight

The wind whispers conspiracy in treetops,
And the gabbling flocks vanish along their flyway
Toward the Gulf. Plump droplets darken shingles
And I cross this threshold where all reverie ends.

THE WATCH

Four yellow roses, one for each month
In our brief season. In September the lawns
Were still emerald, and at night the moon
Ran a shiver of dew through the grass.

The sun scatters fire-opals this morning,
And when the sexton turned his mower
One hundred-eighty degrees it spun out
A wreath at the foot of your blue-veined

Marble. But I remember that October most,
An owl hooded against the frost as it picked
The bones of careless mice, the scent of ripe
Persimmons in the frigid air. You are with me

Even now as you were then, your delicate
Shoulders shaken with laughter, redounding
From vacant carports and the scroll-worked
Eaves of houses we passed along lamplit streets

From Graceland to Paula. By November,
The red and gold leaves of sweetgum maples
Came spinning down like riddled biplanes
And pin-oaks rained acorns on shingled roofs.

We would part in mid-December with no sequel;
You slipped the timepiece from your wrist,
Wordlessly handing it to me. For a quarter-
Century it ticked away with exquisite precision

Keeping the pulse of all the years from that one
To this. What do I have to give you now
But a few hours quiet watch on your lawn
And these fireflies' stone lanterns lighting up?

THE GHOSTLY HEART

Until one of us turned to unregenerate clay,
You vowed that you'd always love me.
My own people lie beneath the satin-lined
Rafters of the Odd Fellows Cemetery

In Greenwood, Mississippi. The immortal
Robert Johnson was slipped a fatal dram
There in 1938, and Furry Lewis who could
Make his guitar fret like a bluebottle fly

Took his gift up to smoke-filled juke joints
In Memphis. One leg severed by a freight
Southbound on those twin ribbons of steel
That meet in infinity, he lived on the third

Floor of a flophouse when I first met him;
He'd play slide for hours with his pocket
Knife of dimpled bone, and we boys would
Listen spellbound by what we'd purchased

For a pint of Ten High whisky. In this Delta
Metropolis, only bluesman W. C. Handy,
Fingering the oily valves of his trumpet,
And Elvis arrested mid-swivel on Beale St.

Have been cast in bronze. Composers
And troubadours of a lesser stamp would
Be obliged to bide their time, hardly aware
That the genuine adept makes the era his

Or her own. I wanted to make your name
A byword for all things of beauty and grace,
Hoping to transcend those street-fights on
Overton Square, the evenings dealing Booray

In the backroom of nightclubs in Natchez.
Longing to win one kiss of salty eroticism
And celestial sweetness from your pert lips,
Teresa, I soon learned such things meant

Nothing unless freely given. I later marveled
How the four months of grace you lavished
On me couldn't be sounded on any keyboard
But were chords struck deep in a ghostly heart.

SOUND WISDOM

To venture that I was familiar with night
On the Delta, would be putting it all
Too mildly. In my late teens a pewter flask
Rode my hip and I tucked in my right boot

An eight-inch blade hafted in dimpled bone.
I didn't court trouble, but knew cemeteries
Were full of coffins, their rubber gaskets
Rotting in the August humidity. Every

Streetlamp smoked like a topaz in a box
Lined with grey felt. I'd conjure you
When I passed the country club
And heard the night watchman sifting

The static on his radio for the Cardinals
Double-header, soothing a quart of Bud,
The egg-salad sandwich and greasy chips
His wife bagged on the table beside him.

Unfamiliar footsteps would raise the hackles
On his Doberman's back, and he'd flick on
His battery-packed flashlight. But he would
Always make the padlock's tumblers ripple

And open up so I could take in a few innings
And talk about women. "Bide your
Time, boy, but don't forget don't none 'em
Mind a man likin' it." He agreed that a nip

Now and then did no harm, "But get rid
Of that gut-fetcher; it's borrowin' trouble,
And she'll likely take you for a hood." He
Had one further admonition: "Death is kin to

A debt-collector; he just wants to get better
Acquainted—he don't necessarily want
To be friends." Perhaps to a lady
These words smack of chawbacon vulgarity,

But I for one number Walt among the ranks
Of the permanently wise. Decades have passed,
And you both rest beneath ledger-stones, names
Scored deeper than mallet and chisel can strike.

THE MACHINERY OF NIGHT

While only a youth I visited the composing
Room of the Memphis *Commercial Appeal*,
Watched the green-hooded lamp illuminate
The old Linotype keyboard that my father's

Beautiful square hands plied so dexterously,
The slugs of hot lead dropping into slots,
The whole mechanism shifting and shuttling
Like a loom singing in Odysseus's great hall.

I had hoped our love would soon eclipse
The bales of printed pulpwood men bucked
Into truck beds below the icy loading dock
Then sped away beneath a blizzard of stars.

But I still remember the pumice-gritty soap
Black with carbon ink in the foaming dish
Above the lavatory sink when I rose for class,
The polyp-ridden snoring of a man who would

Not live to see fifty years of endless nightshifts
Go funneling down the drain into oblivion. I'd
Slide out the oaken bureau drawer, then open
With reverence his snibbed leather kit all

Aglitter with the cult tools of his thwarted calling,
The stemmed mouth mirror and the wicked-hooked
Pick for probing the cusps of molars that otherwise
Twinkle like star sapphires. A scant sixteen months

Short of his DDS a perforated ulcer forced him
To withdraw from the University of Mississippi.
Meanwhile black columns in the Scripps-Howard
Rival *Press-Scimitar* bruited about the summer

Soirees on your patio, fireflies lighting up
Switchboards of honeysuckle vine along the chain-
Link fence, cool breezes winnowing your blue lawn.
I shunned the round of proms, cotillions, and dances,

Yet a certain sovereignty of spirit, as you called it,
Sounded in us a mutual chord, felt-cored hammers
Falling like 1970's autumn leaves, ghostly hands
Rummaging the tuned ivories of the grand piano

On the Hotel Peabody's mezzanine. We met once
After your divorce, dining in their restaurant
On rack of lamb and a fine cabernet. Although
You took it as a matter of course, the sumptuous

Repast set me back a day's pay. Your pearls,
Teresa, took added luster from such radiant
Skin. When I bade you farewell, burly cicadas
High in elms were turning the machinery of night.

THE LETTER

I set out in my father's navy peacoat,
A white Razorback baseball cap
Pulled low over both eyes, my jacket
Collar high, a distillate autumn mist

Stippling the steep sidewalk buckled
By tree roots, the streetlamp's beam
Like the spillage of a broken egg yolk
On the wet pavement beneath my feet.

Oddly, this nightscape in Fayetteville,
Still a provincial college town in 1995,
Awakens in my psyche the felicitous
Dolor of Erik Satie's *Gymnopedies*.

An old friend wrote from Memphis
To disclose ill tidings, how an aneurysm
Exploding like a supernova, ended your
Temporal existence in mid-September.

I mark a great horned owl's soundless
Buffetings as it circles the south tower
Of the Old Main, then lights, shuffling
Its yellow feathers against pelting rain.

Native Americans in the 19th century
Deemed the winged raptor a good omen
In affairs of the heart. Here am I, utterly
Bereft—you were the one girl who ever

Called love out of me in my first youth.
Hurrying past the red-brick edifice, I
Indulge in a nip from my hip flask, an
Old familiar warmth settling into each

Petalled bone. I cross the leaf-strewn
Campus, cut through the cemetery,
Mulling over Dante's *La Vita Nuova*,
Scarcely noticing a diamondback's

Hide shellacked and nailed to the ice-
House door since last August.
Some feckless machete-wielding lad
Doubtless keeps the buttoned rattle

Tucked in his shirt pocket, a talisman
Against bad luck. I could tally on its
Abacus all the years I've lived here
In the listing shadow of Mt. Sequoia.

But tonight, I feel only your
Absence pricked out by fine drizzle,
A chill making both forearms scaly,
And begin my slow descent homeward.

BACKWARD GLANCES

I. Woolgathering

I conceived of you as one who came and went
In many incarnations; others doubtless yielded
To imaginative excess: a striking blonde of 9th
Century Scandinavia, her cloak dyed purple
And pinned with golden disc broaches. She
Wore lightly enough a chatelaine gaudy with
Latchkeys of privilege and rank. But I put
Aside such chimeras before age fifteen. Still,
My own woolgathering persists like ground
Fog in the cotton field across the highway
Before the sun fires one opal in the dew. I
Recall a clarinet player who plied his trade
From Beale Street to Bourbon, dexterously
Fingering the keys, sounding out each note
Along reed, barrel, and bell as his instrument
Cooled down to a few bleak embers. He would
Then take his ease in some sequestered spot off
Stage, sipping a tall schooner of Schlitz. Did
He conjure a girl's fine-boned wrists, delicate
Shoulders, and muscular brown thighs, one
Who baffled his dreams even as he lovingly
Addressed his clarinet's baffle set after set,
Far into endless nights where waitresses moved
Through lounges bearing trays of gin-rickeys
That clink with ice? Better than most he knows
Those pawnshop windows smoking with gems
Wherein rosewood violins cure like hams, and scaly
Iridescent harmonicas bear mute witness to the fact

That blues without reedy wheezing and a little
Honest spit is neither fervent nor earnest. All this
In dream-light growing ever dimmer.

    II. Dark Chambers
Perhaps your great-grandmother like my own
Would strike a match in the predawn dark;
Grafting the little hell-blossom to a lamp wick,
She'd adjust the englobed flame with the twist
Of a brass key. Once she was as lovely as you,
Luxuriating in lavender bath crystals evenings
When the moon's burnished scythe crests high
Above a birch grove; the russet autumn leaves
Whisper like mowers' blades in wind-bent wheat.
Listen to the yellow braid and tassel
Percussing like rain on split-shingled roofs,
The long harvest rows at last fallen all one way.
But let's dismiss these rural idylls now quick only
In the minds of a select few. Return to the notion
Of metropolis from the Cyclopean stone of Mycenae
With its carved heraldic lions and beehive tombs
To the sun-struck glass and steel towers rising
From Manhattan to the Crescent City. It's New
Year's Eve in the Quarter and the ornate filigree
Of second-floor balustrades weeps like metal off
A soldering iron; the baroque scrollwork is crusted
Frosting on a wedding cake. It was a short
Stroll in sleeting rain to Elysian Fields, named
For Paris' *Champs-Élysées*; after dinner you to went
Up to our room, but I lingered at the bar, observing
How the publican poured Drambuie into a shot
Glass like some acolyte lighting a votive nub. I

Followed Prince Charles Edward's drink with two
Slings of Grand Marnier, and, the blue pilot light
In my brain turned low, I mounted the stairs to
Dark chambers where you still wait for all I know.

DECEMBER, 1978

Yet even now I envision it, how you
Winsomely straddled a padded
Vanity stool before your gilt-framed
Bedroom looking-glass, and myself

Struck dumb with adoration at you
Fingering each faceted jewel barbed
Like a hook in some angler's three-
Tiered tackle box. Billiard parlor

Rubes labeled you jail-bait, but I
Felt an unremitting wonder as you
Fitted each earlobe with sparkling
Sapphire studs. I imagined you

Sporting brown saddle oxfords
Those cool Delta daybreaks, mint-
Scented breath blooming as you
Traipsed daintily along beneath

Oaks pyrotechnic with fall color.
Already late for first period, you
Listened for the bell to ring like
An ax-blade on a honing wheel.

All this while I deftly downshifted
And my eight-cylinder Olds bucked
Low, waiting for the traffic signal to
Flip from red to amber and the hue

Akin to Gatsby's blue lawn. Mornings,
I motored by my former two-bedroom
"Crackerbox" on South Prescott, hell-
Bent for the University of Memphis,

The lecture halls where I met Chaucer,
Shakespeare, Donne, Keats, Hopkins,
And the whiskey-fueled Welshman who
Still labors by singing light. In less than

A twelfth-month, we quietly commenced
Mid-September our autumn dalliance,
Parting when shingle roofs in Graceland
Swarmed with splinters of Yuletide frost.

Brandied fruitcakes squinting raisins
Were sliced with trowel-bladed knives
On teak sideboards from Elvis Presley
Boulevard to Millbranch Road, rich

Confection hefted in ample bricks toward
Dining-room tables. Blue firs twinkled
Glass-blown globes, and I fancied myself
An impoverished youth, his nose pressed

To a casement flowering with ice. Four
Months I languished in precious agony,
Mimicking Yuri Zhivago in Pasternak's
Epic. But April dawned deliquescent,

Lacy glaze melting in a slather down
Cottage panes. Neither morose nor

Remorseful, I awakened to measures
Enchanting as electrons and neutrons

Dancing around a stable nucleus like
Angels on the head of a pin.
We met again at the public library's
Card catalogue, ink a quivering dew

On your divorce decree. Twenty-five
Proved so magical in you. The luster
Of girlhood remained, but your soul's
Depth and understanding were new.

Then I ceased to pass nights laboring
Over an old Underwood's onyx keys,
Or bathed in a television's cathode rays
While I sipped shots of vodka and lime.

We cruised the swank blues joints
And every café on Beale Street, listened
To B. B. King manipulating his six-string;
Bending notes and big with diminishes,

His slick dexterity picked its soulful way
Into legend. We raised glasses to Handy,
The Killer rummaging the banked ivories
Of his 88, Elvis sleeping beneath cold turf

In the shade of his pillared estate. I could
Divine in the crescent moon lost in cirrus
Mist the smooth contour of your cheek.
Unlike the Gypsy in Lorca's *Romancero*

Gitano, I had no need to divest my person
Of an oily chambered revolver and holster
Hand-tooled in black Spanish leather.
We parted forever beneath the marquee

Of Playhouse on the Square, neon tubes
Scribbling in red, blue, and gold cursive
The current feature across S. Cooper's
Rain-slick asphalt, the evening's fare

Dished and wobbling in a taxi's wake
As it regally slides into yet another year.

NARCISSUS TO THE MUSE

Lord, I did lay concern on myself lathering up
With mint-scented soap-on-a-rope, steam rising
From the tile floor, the spindrift suds sucked down
The swirling shower drain. I then drew aside

On tintinnabulating rings the yellow curtain,
Groping for the means to towel off and slip on
My terry-cloth bathrobe. Sweat trickled down
The medicine cabinet mirror until my face

Rode up in the mercury-backed glass. I switched
On the Conair dryer, spellbound as my red-gold
Princeton haircut filled out in thick layers. No need
At fifteen for the Gillette platinum-edged blades,

I smeared English Leather like a heady balm
On my chest yet smooth as the tabula rasa.
It was for you that I put on the pleated
Oxford cloth shirt with the button-down collar,

Navy blue Levis and matching Gold Cup socks,
Then stepped into the oxblood penny loafers
With beef rolls. I shrugged on my wool cardigan
Still crackling with static this October morning

Over a half-century later in the year 2020.
Even before those days strolling HHS corridors
I remember turning the lighted dial of a radio
Surfing burbles and squeaks for the desired AM

Frequency breaking deep in the heart of the Delta.
I imagined Ty Cobb hearthside in the off-season,
The pine log sputtering and resin seething out,
How he lovingly rubbed with oily porkchop bones

His bat of tight-grained maple to prevent chipping.
When its barrel connected, he could feel the tingling
Recoil in his palms and watch the horsehide pill's
Slow trajectory toward the rising tide in the bleachers.

When I toed the rubber in the junior-league,
The new-mown infield grass was more emerald
Than diamond. Every time I kicked and fired
I studied the physics of grip, pressure, release,

The red stitching on the ball like a Homeric
Figure of eight shield. I was king of the hill,
And bided my time, handling the rosin-bag
Like a leather pouch bulging with gold-dust.

Unable to run my two-seam cutter over 88 m.p.h.,
I chipped at the strike-zone like a dark casement.
Batters would whiff too late a humming fastball
Turning into a wicked slider with my last-second

Flick of the wrist as the white spheroid rolled
Off my fingertips, and I bore the burden lightly
When sluggers swung, both knees buckling,
And muttering curses through the cured leaf,

Flung their helmets and returned to the dugout.
And don't forget the knuckle-bull rotating only once

In sixty and ½ feet around its cushion-cork center
Like a fisherman's cane pole and float hoping

The over-eager hitter would bite and go under.
I was aces too when it came to snagging
Line-drives hit back to the pitcher's mound,
My glove of Italian leather, web, palm, and heel,

Its lacing like the braid and tassel of harvest wheat,
The hinge kneaded dark with neat's foot oil,
Just the thing for hawking blue darters mid-air
And doubling-off some yokel headed for second.

Seldom did I hit a pitch beyond the infield,
But I could lay down a slow roller toward third
And round the bag in a spiked flurry before
The opposing catcher pounced and threw down,

Rifling the ball past the first baseman's mitt
Into right field. I stole home four times that season,
Loitering until some idiot lobbed the ball back
To his battery-mate without leaving his crouch

And I sprinted for the dish at a 4.32 clip,
Obliged to slide only once, the umpire's arms
Spread wide while the dust settled in titters
And the home crowd booed lustily all the while.

But by twelve I'd begun to envy upperclassmen
Punting pebble-grained pigskins in the bricky mid-
November air, those leather-sleeved jackets
Worn only by varsity stalwarts with the letter H

Sewn over their hearts, plus green chevrons
Like high-flying geese to signify captains.
A pastoral sport to be sure, and cheerleaders
Such as you with your blonde Gypsy shag

Caught up in gymnastics and choreographed dance,
Brass tubas pumping out "Georgy Girl," to a flute's
Lilting stops. But our new football Americain
Made the push and pull of the rugby scrum tame,

Hardly the gut-thumping whump like a dozen
Umbrellas exploding along the scrimmage line.
If you listened you could hear shoulder pads pop
In the press box, the exchange of helmet paint

A smudge of pride in locker rooms from Whitehaven
To Bartlett. Then it was legal to chop-block,
Crack-back, horse-collar, and spear-tackling
Was the norm. It led to ruptured knee cartilage,

Torn ligaments, deep-thigh bruises, and concussed
Skulls. One September night under the lights
At Halle Stadium I rushed for 132 yards, my right
Thumb and ring finger fractured when linebackers

Put their Riddell helmets with multibar face masks
Through the ball I was coached to cradle in both arms.
Thus, the hammered gold band you reluctantly
Bestowed on him would never have fit me.

Perhaps you still quicken that dark room silhouetted
Against a canvas screen pulled down like a shade where

Those 16 MM celluloid frames depict Viking exploits
Unfolding to the school projector's slow inexorable roll.

From the ruck and maul of our humanity, those piled limbs
Blown dead by a referee's whistle, we rise incorruptible,
Jumped up and come set again like a band of demons
Doomed to perpetual reenactment by reels run in reverse.

In those days long before overtime you'll not recall
How we went 6-2-2 that season, the team's collective
Fate held up as a warning to others by our taskmaster.
We bled in technicolor beneath those Friday night lights

And were consigned to a vault in black and white.
I came back three years later to watch from the track
You straying impassioned along the sidelines. Perhaps
Some disaffection akin to my own was even then moving

Through you like an unbidden joy. My hair cascaded
To my shoulders, my shirt opened at the throat. I wore
Brown corduroy bell-bottoms over brass-buckled boots.
I was drunk on apple wine, and you looked at me so.

TWO PARABLES

I often remember my father's people,
Their corner grocery on Rayburn St.
In south Memphis, the store's façade
Concrete, how the dead rust undulant
Siding painted aluminum cast a glare
Like water on the tiger lilies trembling
In the banked yard shored and buoyed up
By the beams of railroad ties. Cinders littered
The small lot and August nights bottles
Got busted, somebody cut. Emerald
Shards glittered malign as the fixed gaze
Of a stray cat. Dark lettering read: "Cold
Beer," "Snacks," "Soda," "No Loitering."
Among the heart-shaped catalpa leaves
Cicadas chattered like pressure cookers.
My grandfather behind his counter rang up
Variations deft as any metrical register,
Falstaff from the cooler, Dutch Masters
Panetelas, each empty box that I filled
With colorful lead soldiers an aromatic
Humidor. My sister would slip the bands
Of metallic foil on her fingers, seeking
The perfect fit. With a certain brawn
And swagger, the old man would
Stand to his round stump butcher's block,
Chopping blood sausage and liverwurst
Dubbed "goose liver" by his black customers.
But I loved Sundays when he closed up
At noon; somewhere a radio evangelist

Declaimed with a meetinghouse fervor,
And out back we'd rupture the casks
Of watermelon sunk in a washtub chock
Full of ice. I'd spit out seeds embedded
In the red fruit, black index notches
Of the *Oxford English Dictionary*;
Even then, the word-hoard seemed
Ripe for plunder. My lovely mother,
During her earliest years, resembled you.
Each morning she'd court the calliope
Hummingbird with its purple gorget;
It siphoned nectar from a honeysuckle's
Tiny floral Victrola, its choral wheedling
A blur amid bee balm and sage. The male
Weighs less than the star of a penny
Bright with rheum. The female constructs
Her nest out of a spider's spun gossamer.
Reared in a house on Grand Boulevard
In Greenwood, Mississippi, my maternal
Grandfather primed his rage with bonded
Whiskey. He loved to roll the bones, to shoot
The jive with dock-hands behind the Quinn
Drug Co. A blue .38 riding his hip, he passed
The collection plate odd Sundays, blackjack
Tucked in his breast pocket. Some devout
Church-goers whispered how a white hood
And sheet haunted his bedroom closet.
Oblivious to such rumors my mother
Went serenely about her daily rounds,
Sun cresting the hemlocks, mist burning
Off the lawn in fiery opalescent tints.

NIGHTHAWKS

I. The Rayburn Street Grocery
My grandfather's broad leather strap
Served to strop his straight-edge razor
And polish my butt when I got out-of-line.
He broke the night-long fast with biscuits
Thick as his gold pocket watch, sourdough
Gravy and blood sausage. Lean, blinking
Behind wire-rimmed spectacles, one regular
Customer in the old man's shop swore he
Ate so much "It made him po' to carry it."
During high school he was state champion
In Mississippi's high-jump, then spent
Five years as a relief-pitcher for St. Louis
While they were still called the Browns.
His later years were cast in sepia tones.
In his broad-band fedora he resembled
A slumped figure in Edward Hopper's
Nighthawks, the stark oil on canvas
Depiction of film noir figures in a diner,
Napkin dispensers on the counter, coffee
Tanks in the background, porcelain mugs
Awaiting glazed sinkers our generation
Dubbed doughnuts. Hopper's brooding
Composition requires no "voice over"
Or the various subtitles I rehearse here.

II. The Brister Library Tower
Clerks in the University of Memphis library,
Richard Crowson and I would engage daily

In verbal badinage. Even before sketching
His name into the pages of the *Jackson Sun*
And the *Wichita Eagle*, he remarked to me
With a smart drollery how his "poetry phase"
Had ended at eighteen. My rejoinder
Delineated the boredom of drawing "Heckle
And Jeckle" on deckle-edged butcher paper
From my grandfather's meat locker before
I turned six. Still, I peered in when old
"Ricky the Crow" opened his musty text
To Dürer's *Knight, Death, and the Devil,*
And he'd listen to me recite "Byzantium"
By the restless warden of Thoor Ballylee.

    III. The Daily Round

My father's mother baked cornbread
Apportioned in thick-sliced wedges;
Ringing up purchases on the register
While my grandfather napped, she'd
Daub at various pigments come evening.
Although she never finished high school,
A certain fluency guided the sure dip
And glide of her bristled horsehair brush
As a red barnlike timber-truss bridge
Spanning a blue stream would converge
On plain cotton smelling of linseed oil.
Once an art dealer chanced on the store,
But she claimed her paintings were too
Poor to sell and too dear to give away.
Her genuine avocation was the canning
Of blackberry preserves: "bramble-jam"

As the neighbors would have it. My own
Mother, who measured out her girlhood
With a sterling silver sugar shell,
Declared it talent squandered on a man
Whose sole concern was the daily round.
Resettling the dent in his hat, the old gent
Would shrug on his grey trench coat and
Vanish into October's early morning fog.

ANOTHER REALM OF DISCOURSE

I. My Father's Household
As a youth, my father devoured flannel
Cakes mauled in blackstrap molasses, an
Electric percolator's cover knob rattling
Like a lone brown penny spun heads up
On a wooden counter. His grandmother
Dipped snuff, and the repurposed blue
Maxwell House can chimed like a barber
Shop cuspidor. Buttered potatoes sweeter
Than the notes of an ocarina graced most
Depression-era supper tables. Piping hot,
A yam often bore the mark of the spade
In its orange skin. Soon my father's pores
Squinted like accordion beads beneath
The blazing sun at Peleliu and Tarawa.
I still own the bolt-action rifle he took off
A Japanese Imperial Marine he killed
In the heat-refracted nightmare of single
Combat. An amphibious soldier's only
Respite lay in cracking open a cold quart
Of Falstaff. The amber bottle's lip fumed
As he slaked in humidity for all the world
Akin to the Mississippi Delta in August.

II. My Mother's Schooling
You are always first to enter my mind
Every time I recall my mother's text on
Etiquette purchased at Mississippi State
College for Women. Never mind the house
Wine be it crackling Italian red intended

To accompany bread and brie or an ice-
Hot Chardonnay served by the carafe.
She told me to observe the cork's brand,
Its frail hermetic scrimshaw, whenever
Sommelier or steward broaches a bottle,
And always to sniff for any hint of taint.
Neither gourmand nor tosspot, I noted
Scrupulously each wine glass: base,
Stem, bowl, and rim. I often longed
To trace the ruby, amber-lit claret's
Translucence to its roots in the Latin
Claritas or a vineyard's cultivated rows.
Like you, I preferred the sacraments
Of sun and soil, eschewing the impulse
To filter these through the high artifice
Of institutional adornment such as light
Staining the windows at Saint Chappell.

    III. Coda

Our generation endowed the locution
"Plastic" with a negative resonance. We did
Not recall that it derives from the Greek: *plassein*
"To shape or mold." How many lyrics spun
Out of 33 r.p.m. discs awakened in us strains
Haunting as The Beatles' "Long and Winding
Road," the molten gold and plangent loveliness
Of Elvis' "It's Now or Never"? Can we forget
Gladys Knight's rendering of "Midnight Train
To Georgia" penned by Ole Miss quarterback
Jim Weatherly? The wine list was least
On my mind seated opposite you one last time
That rain-swept evening in April. Moistening
Your lower lip, you knew I couldn't forgo a taste.

SELF-FASHIONING

I. Origins
I still recall when I was five years old
That first summer we lived on South
Prescott in Memphis; we had no AC
And slept under blades of an oscillating
Fan, arms and legs smeared with cool
Lotion, even as the thermometer's bleb
Threatened to pop and the sickle moon
Quivered in droplets silvering green-
Leafed grass on the new-mown lawn.
The previous noon road crews paved
The wide thoroughfare, the sun's glad
Tuba pumping out tar bubbles we burst
With sticks in the sweltering heat. Come
Dark, the older boys stole smudge pots
Or "cannonballs" meant to light road
Construction, hurling them sputtering
Like grenades through the twilight air.
The nocturnal tableau awakens in me
Tchaikovsky's *1812 Overture*, as T-
Shirted and denim-overhauled youths
Cavorted to rumbling kettledrums before
Slipping the snares of outraged adults.
My favorite interlude came three hours
Before when I wolfed curbside vanilla ice-
Cream coated with chocolate, five cents
A bar, purchased from a van resembling
An ambulance and passing to the tinkle
And whir of a miniature carillon. Four

Years later came the move to Whitehaven,
The droning window-unit in my parents'
Bedroom, and the pallet I spread beneath,
Turning evenings into refrigerated sleep.

II. Interlude
A desolate man could walk right into those
Smoldering grey-blue eyes, black brows
Behind which it seemed no countenance
Could scheme. Your honey-blonde hair
Could embrace the nestlings of a Sappho
Comet hummingbird. Your upper lip's
Philtrum set my collarbones ringing years
Before these airy conceits blazed their way
Into my lyric cosmology. My namesake
For Genesis divined our love's crescendo
Building along the Delta's night skyline
A decade after the fact. Soon I'd track
Lambent headlamp beams over the Boston
Mountains toward Fayetteville, Arkansas.

III. Singing School
I arrived at the University of Arkansas
Intent on an MFA in Creative Writing;
A critically acclaimed slender volume
Of poetry to my name, in some measure
I craved the school's validation for skills
Smoothly assumed I already possessed.
I came for verses and luckily got chapter
And book into the bargain. Enduring
The tedium of workshop, I hankered after
The ghost of Frank Stanford. Mississippi

Delta and Ozark prodigy, he appeared then
A sanctified singer, a lost soul who declaimed
With a meetinghouse fervor. He chanted
About the full moon swollen blue as a tick
On a bloodhound's ear, a levee worker's
Smoked lunch meat, the young girl's nest
Of spicery trickling when she bathed naked
In Banjo Creek. Lines baited with minnows,
He snagged channel cat on the hook of native
Wit and one dusk lay down on an iron-framed
Feather bed, banging off into his heart three
Rounds from a .22 caliber target pistol with
Imitation pearl grips. Big Jim Whitehead said
Death and pretty ladies were his ruination,
Urging as a warning to me Stanford's fate.

IV. The Graduate Assistant
I stood at the podium before my students three
Mornings each week, my legal pad color-coded
In calligraphic loops and swirls flowing into
Lectures prepared days in advance. I made
My entrance with the old man's navy peacoat
Designed for World War II draped strategically
Over my left shoulder, a pastel blue scarf like
A Lutheran stole hanging about my neck. My
Pinstripe shirt with heavy starch in buttoned-
Down collar and cuffs wilted as my Seiko ticked
Away the allotted ninety minutes. I strove to be
An amiable charismatic but there lurked within
A smug taskmaster who did not give but assigned
Grades. Across a broad board of green slate
I blocked out in yellow chalk topics for the next
Period of lecture and prolonged, vigorous debate.

V. Arrival

I deemed myself akin to the priest in Lennon
And McCartney's "Eleanor Rigby," but little
Guessed the full compass of love's lonely and
Austere offices until attaining the elusive PhD.
While a student I resorted to home remedies
Like chicory and queen bee honey for a sore
Throat. Now I could afford a penicillin shot
But prescriptions remained high as a bristling
Cat's back. The department chair demanded
A new book of poetry or critical prose every
Fifth year; self-medicating on plump dollops
Of Chivas Regal scotch was quite typical.
Delineating the intersection of East and West,
I cited the Macedonian and the Nazarene as
Exemplars of the Hellenistic world. Alexander,
Fortified by the Oracle at Delphi, chopped
The Gordian knot and rode in pomp to Babylon.
The Magi followed a comet hovering above
The hayricks and outlying stables of Bethlehem
Ephrata. The pagan Greek was Apollonian,
Whereas the Redeemer always comes a dark way.
The risen Christ consumed fish and a honeycomb's
Waxwork mosaic charged with sweetness to prove
He was no ghost to his frighted disciples. Alexander's
Corpse, embalmed in a rich sarcophagus glutted
With liquid gold, endured until Caesar Augustus
Caressed its face, flaking off a piece of the nose.
The ancients believed that honey imparts eloquence:
Thus, I've eaten my due portion in the sure and certain
Hope these lines will abide until an inevitable terminus.

WAVELENGTHS

I. Predawn Quest

Before dawn colors the horizon I awake,
Watching stars congeal to signs any soul
Might deem auspicious; regarding starry
Leaves of sweetgum maple, its cork stems
Sealed by barbed frost, setting the land-
Scape ablaze with rich autumnal hues, I
Still recall the old "cracker box" house
On South Prescott and its upright radio:
Electric sap seemed to burble and squeak
As I turned the knob searching for just
The right frequency on our antique Philco,
Its art deco cabinet resembling New York's
Chrysler building, swank lobby adorned
With amber, onyx, and marble. I shunned
The big band orchestral strains
For Cannonball Adderly's barreling sax,
All the hungry rock and roll artists cutting
Sides on the Sun and Stax labels right here
In Memphis. Elvis Presley, Little Richard,
And Jerry Lee Lewis plugged into juke joints
Of neon red, blue, and gold, were quaking
Ramshackle barbeque dives from Beale St.
To Old Highway 51. One October afternoon
At my grandparents' Rayburn Street grocery
Afforded ample 90 proof how hard it was for
The other side to "get over," a poor neighbor-
Hood where feckless men with no intention
Of paying midwives who birthed their brood

Were often branded with the opprobrium,
"Granny-Dodger." Yet the specter of Elvis
Sporting the piped braid of a Loew's State
Usher, another "Humes High greaser" who
Would graduate to down-shifting his Crown
Electric two-door on slow grades between
Tupelo and Nashville, inspired every Delta
Lyricist to pursue those reflecting lines zipping
By like tracer bullets on darkened highways.

II. Legacies of Loss
Always it seems I return to Memphis'
Once and future "King," his hair pomaded
With rose oil and Vaseline, Ace comb tracks
Shining like outsized record grooves. My folks
Would let me stay all night on Rayburn St.
While they watched Elvis play the Overton
Park Shell in the evenings; those early gigs
Accreted like pearls Col. Tom Parker lovingly
Cultivated while groundskeepers mopped
Urine gushed in the aisles by enraptured
Teenage girls. Presley would work the ache
Of a fretted six-string into callused fingers,
Crooning "Love Me Tender," before he broke
Into hip-gyrating rhythms, and the soulful
Wail of "Jailhouse Rock." It was a full decade
Before another King would be coolly dialed up
Into a rifle scope's crosshairs and nailed while
Leaning on the Lorrainne Motel's second-floor
Railing. I little realized then we had inherited
A legacy of loss greater than we could dream.

III. The Reckoning

You and I grew to maturity while the lads
From Liverpool were at floodtide; The Beatles
Disbanded by the time we paired off, their mantra
Of love not lost on us. Our day-to-day assignations
Were curiously nocturnal but didn't preclude
The dawn rendezvous when everything seems
Birth-wet and new and delight resides in pure
Anticipation. But didn't George Harrison insist
"All Things Must Pass" and you knew it must
Be so well before I did; our first parting occurred
In a small café the morning of December 14, 1970.
Somewhere I'm still sifting that old radio dial
In the predawn dark pricked out with stars
For some wavelength bearing me home to you.

LATE CHRONICLES

I. Back Pages
Here it all begins with those idyllic summers
Cherished for their remoteness but familiar
As an exercise in composition of place; I delve
Into my past smoothly as Nellie Bruce dipped her
Ice-cream scoop into a half-gallon of frozen
Strawberry confection, plopping concupiscent
Dollops into porcelain bowls. Then she shooed
Us out the kitchen door to sit in a mimosa's
Shade and avidly partake, blithely unaware
That the ancients deemed red fruit exclusively
The food of the dead. Could Winfred and I
Conceive in that hour how we are all creatures
Of time and fate? Only I glimpsed mantis eggs
Clinging to the tree's bole like the thorax
Of a Greek hoplite's breast plate. Soon the pod
Would hatch and disgorge carnivorous mites
Maturing into born killers, their triangular
Heads mounted to a revolving swivel. Stilted
Chartreuse exoskeletons case-hard with terrible
Hooked forearms, they could crush a cricket's
Husk before it took up its crepuscular fiddling.
I pinched between my thumb and forefinger
One of those green predators a quarter-century
Later and marveled how its grip was stronger
Than the latch to the screen door we urchins
Heard clap behind us so long ago. No wonder
These voracious insects even preyed on geckos.
I'd read in my teens how the female devours

Her mate during copulation and shrugged,
Recalling that age when all song was prayer.
Mid-November's chill popped the cardboard
Stoppers of milk bottles on front porches
All along South Prescott even as I slumbered
Under my grandmother's satin-patched quilt.

II. Forging On

Sometimes in one breath I wake to hollow tones
Of the courthouse clock, a bronze bell tonguing
Twelve in the tower above its lighted dial. No
Shadows lengthen the Confederate statues hewn
Out of marble with lapidary strokes. Black elms
Line the boulevard where I listen for the cicada
Clack of my grandmother's treadle-driven antique
Singer hymning satin oddments into the dazzling
Counterpane I slept beneath when autumnal
Frost swarmed like quartz and froze white quarts
Ranged on our doorstep before we could broach
And pour their sweet concord over breakfast flakes.
I conjure when hand-carved gourds lit up
By purple votive nubs supplanted those bottles
On thresholds and our season of leaves and masks
Hurrying marked an era before gumdrops tinct
With LSD and grenade apples bristling razorblade
Shrapnel were dropped in brown paper bags. Lord
Help puckish hobgoblins now touching the doorbell's
Luminous pip, unaware of the maimed psyche
Skulking inside. Behind my grandfather's corner
Grocery I would happen on the Thanksgiving
Turkey's claws like dragon scales, and ponder
The severed head's vacant eye unable to conceive

That the old man was someone to flee. Imagining
The blue hatchet's abrupt stroke was real enough
For me. In less than a fortnight the first flakes
Will break into crystal high above the moonlit
Spires of spruce and fir across the highway
From this four-room cinderblock house wherein
I now weather sleepless evenings without you.
Embarked on my eighth decade, I languidly dip
A golden nib, replenish my glass of vodka and lime.

DUAL ALLEGORIES

I. Departure: 1970

Only in haunting dreams do I behold
The Byzantine cut of your gaze recast
In shades of limpid blue and yet recall
The profligate life I led after we parted.
Summer nights I doled out U.S. currency,
A dollar bill's intimate cotton and linen
Weave just so much fodder for asserting
One's masculine bravura on a theater's
Verge as I paid wages freighted with sin,
Watching banty roosters lean-thewed
And muscular, bred for the pit and fitted
With steel spurs to facilitate the kill. Men
Born in the Delta listen for a fighting-cock's
Wishbone struck like a tuning fork, that
Black chord resonant in the blood, a sticky
Infusion animating our corporeal selves.
I read Frank Stanford's *The Battlefield*
Where the Moon Says I Love You each night.
On the back porch I'd give the mouth harp
A wavering blast. His answer drifted back
From cropper's fields vanished long ago,
A train bearing his coffin, bound for a remote
Station of the Southern Cross. It carried also
Tipplers of Four Roses blended bourbon,
Moonlight gamblers, and midnight ramblers.
Others boarded: cigar-tokers, big-time jokers,
All late-hour flesh-defilers, their own plus
The heretofore sanctified carcasses of others.

II. Renewal: 1978

You embodied a largesse of soul,
Upon which I cannot hope to look again.
I remember the breakfast nook provided
With buttermilk biscuits and apple butter;
Cheese croissants accompanied artichoke
Hearts at lunch. We dined evenings off
Overton Square, smoked pork-shoulder
And Pinot Noir vintage 1973, its blood
Deep in the storied lineage of kings. But
Even during our renewed halcyon days
I dreamed about toads in a baptismal font.
I imagined stringing lyre-shaped horns
From an arrow-stricken antelope skewered
On the Serengeti plain and yearned after
The lyric's untrammeled power to celebrate
And subvert. I hearkened to the muffled
Drumming of ghetto Cadillacs, dashboards
Thundering as the Supremes' Jean Terrell
Belted out "Stoned Love," bearing Motown's
Label into new era. I could blithely conceive
Some DJ threading each disc like a needle
With a sledge-hammer. However, I cherished
Even more the dark comeliness of your speech,
The way you nurtured the least syllable
Like a precious ember on the tongue. All my
Lingual cunning and knack for *tableau vivant*
Seemed but risqué indulgences at that hour.
I listen now for dark avowals of your heart.

A LAPSED PAEAN

I. Carving as an Art

Doubtless this paean will seem wanting in amorous
Design but each phrasal turn hews to the contours
Of the numinous while trusting the mystery to arise
From the commonplace. We root our jack o'lanterns
In Celtic lore, a grimace gouged in a turnip's purple,
Lit within by embers to guide errant souls at night
Through peat bogs and murky fens. Fluent, dipping
Knives such as we used to core pumpkins thumped
For ripeness in grocery stores were honed to a lethal
Niceness and pocketed in macs flapping all along
The docks and quays of Ulster. One conjures the mein
Of those nocturnal wayfarers florid with potations
And despair fueled by more than the national tuber.
The Delta's greenish phosphor called foxfire
From the Old French *faux* or "fox" dwells in rotten
Cypress stumps. It awakens childhood memories
Of the lighted clock dial on the funeral home lawn
In Greenwood, Mississippi. But I return to my homely
Trope, reflecting on an ice-sculpture the dissolute
Pietro de Medici required of Michelangelo, a Virgin
And Child reduced to slush once the sun gained its
Meridian, the sublime genius and master spirit
Of Renaissance Italy humbled by an ephemeral
Odd job one morning when Florence lay beneath
A marmoreal splendor evoking the precipitous
Cliffs above Carrara. T.S. Eliot declared poetry
"A mug's game," but Doctor Samuel Johnson
Observed that the true merit of Buonarroti's art

Slumbered in its medium: "Sir, we would not offer
A farthing for the same head carved upon a carrot."

    II. The Sculptor's Craft
Stalwart quarrymen during the Quattrocento labored
To shear *la pietra della luce* or "the stone of light" free
From that storied peak in Tuscany. They hammered
With iron sledges tiered wooden wedges into marble
Then saturated the timber stakes with water. These
Expanded and the precious rock calved like a glacier.
More than one polished slab fell beneath the knowing
Hand of Michelangelo who insisted the Saint Peter's
Basilica *Pietà* depicting Christ tackled down from cross-
Beams still sweating resin and laid across a pubescent
Virgin's lap already slept in marble. It required only
His visionary genius to crack the formula and release
The divine tableau. Remember me as one who
Pounded an old Underwood's keyboard until 3 a.m.
All summer in 1972, a youth moved by your cheeks'
Contour, the subtly in every caress, and laughter-
Loving eyes—how I yearned to catch your essence
As I respooled battered ribbons one by one, desperate
To strike it rich beyond the linear black. Every night
The creek by the cemetery braided and stitched; I
Imagined owls winking like lanterns in the woods.
Before morning fog burned off McKellar Lake's
Placid surface I heard a drake rise and go spanking
Low over tufted bullrushes nodding in the shallows.
I recalled netting tadpoles wriggling like quarter notes
Among iridescent reeds as a child. But always my
Reveries return to you, and the magisterial
Figured of aged Michelangelo huddled near a fireplace

Where embers shift and glow, his brimming noggin
Of brandy kept warm with a hot poker. He knew:

III. Fresco: An Elusive Beauty

Carbon ticks once in a thousand years; all the while
My typewriter's lapidary strokes aimed for a diamond
Luster. Yet I realized that even the ultimate maestro
Who earned the honorific *Il Divino* during his lifetime
Bridled at Pope Julius's commission to set blazing
With rich pigment the Sistine Chapel ceiling. No chiseled
Equestrian statue's plunging stallion could have been
More fractious than this sculptor who felt "drowned
In paint." Four years he lay on a scaffold and toiled
By a candle beading its wax rosary into the wee hours;
Yeats put it best: "With no more sound than the mice
Make / His hand moves to and fro." Buonarroti pricked
Holes into each cartoon and sprayed it with coal dust,
Outlines transferred onto wet plaster and then adorned
In lustrous hues. His method proved the origin
Of dot matrix, a technology I shunned for the chattering
Ball of an IBM Selectric. But what eludes me is the knack
For portraiture of any kind, the gift to frieze in due time
The ineffable lovliness of our interlude still fresh in my mind.

POTENT LIBATIONS

I. The Green Fairy
Like a jazz pianist reaching inside
Each key for the notes, I longed to sound
Ghostly tonal felicities quick within us all
Those years ago. But now my music seems
Scored like wormwood. In autumn, 1970,
We met once in a dimly lit café to imbibe
Absinthe, "the green fairy," concocted
During la Belle Epoch along the Seine
In an era when idle legionnaires pursued
Goose-girls up hayricks. Then Cézanne
Wielded the palate-knife without stint;
Van Gough's *Starry Night* rained oils
On a cobalt-blue sky swarming celestial
Orbs in palpable Indian yellow. Tête-à-tête,
We set about our ritual; I deftly placed
One sugar cube on a spatulate silver spoon,
Next pouring an ounce of *la fee verte* through
The confection into a stemmed glass. I'd scratch
Flame from a matchhead and light granules
Tinct with absinthe until they caramelized.
A carafe of ice-water followed and we carelessly
Sipped the 70% alcohol, savoring not the least
Of black licorice. I was a strapping lad aged
Eighteen; still my father would've raised welts
Across my back with stropped leather only two
Years before. He could make such stripes sing
Like larks. But then you and I dissolved
In a neuro-reactive bliss, heedless of any desire

For orange sunshine or purple microdot. No tale
About Lot's wife turned into a wrath-solid pillar
Of salt could prevail on us to look back or regret
Our sole indulgence by flickering candlelight.

    II. Another Libation
Born November 4th 1951, a blue plastic
Capsule with a paper strip inscribed thirty-
Nine ordained my slot in the Vietnam death-
Lottery. Determined not to allow the ill-luck
Of the draw to airlift me to the Mekong Delta
Or the hills around Pleiku, I kept my grade
Point average at Memphis State well above
3.00. Others fled to Quebec and Toronto,
Shunned rifle platoons and mortar-teams
Lobbing shells into bamboo villages thatched
With reeds. While I learned how Helen burnt
The topless towers of Ilium, marines fired hovels
Belonging to "zipperheads" with Zippo lighters
Ignited by little spark wheels and flint. Mean-
While black youths from the inner city suffered
Conscription in droves and McGuire's "Eve
Of Destruction" shook every tenement radio.
Dressed in an emerald cheerleader's
Skirt, you seemed "the green fairy" in your
Very person, blonde shag sculpted at the hands
Of a salon stylist. Autumn leaves blazed red
And gold; you were to me a heady intoxicant,
A dram spiced with nutmeg and cinnamon,
The season's living embodiment needing none
Of the stealthy cachet bestowed by potions
Quaffed in a café alcove so many decades ago.

ELUSIVE COUPLINGS

I. Grand Boulevard

My earliest memories have taproots deep
In Greenwood, Mississippi's rich Delta soil,
My mother's hometown where barns burst
With cotton ginned and carded in the year
Of my birth, 1951. Named for the Choctaw's
Last great chieftain, Leflore County's small
Abode teemed with buyers dealing in the cash
Crop, stud poker, bonded whisky, and onyx-
Eyed lovelies in the bustling red-light district
South of the Yazoo River bridge. Engineers
Guiding the Columbus and Greenville line
Diesels tugged on their brass-mounted horns
And waved to me; but I dreamed of old coal-
Burning locomotives freighting picked bolls
To all points of the compass, smoke batting
Their tall stacks. I often imagined fabulous
Throttlemen tapping at valves and meters,
Wrenches clinking, even as I tinker with
This faltering metric. Perhaps years later,
A weary girl fitfully sleeping beneath silk
Sheets, you sensed a train's slow passing
By the tremor in cabinets filled with amethyst
And crystal. Then it seemed chuffing iron
Horses traveled more on wine glasses than
Steel rails burnished smooth by gliding tons.

II. Rayburn Street

My father's parents opened the Rayburn St.
Corner grocery in Memphis five years later;

Derelict crossties shored the side yard's steep
Embankment heaped with cinders. Shards
Of broken beer bottles shone like bright topaz
Scattered in some slag heap. Railroad tracks
Ran a quarter-mile to the south and grandma
Would fix lunch for hoboes—thick pork chops
And french fries—who knocked at her kitchen
Door. They would often chalk an angel curbside
As a signal to fellow bindlestiffs. A retired switch-
Man, Mr. Linten would lean on the red cooler
August nights and swig a chill quart of Falstaff.
Seersucker cap pushed back on his forehead,
He'd take his pocket watch from its trickling
Gold chain and let me examine it for hours.
Consumption carried him off one day
Holding fast to my grandfather's hand. Once
I'd seen the change of ten summers I flattened
Minted coppers under the grinding wheels
Of the Illinois Central, but the black youths
I sorted with called me a fool because a penny
Redeemed two crème-filled cookies in the store.
I little understood the bleak necessities of want
Or those small pleasures that must attend them.

III. Our Own Couplings
No station or roundhouse came with the Lionel
Train set circa. 1961 I got for Christmas several
Months before. But I hearkened to the clack
Of what dawned on me were mattress springs
Bearing my parents away in the bedroom next
My own when I was an infant. Red lanterns
Swinging from the caboose receded as I drifted

Into slumber. Not a soul listened for our own
Lovemaking's low commotion a decade later.
Teresa, we dined on chicken cordon bleu
In the evening and popped the cork on a bottle
Of excellent chardonnay before climbing stairs
To find our mutual appetites merely whetted
For elusive couplings forever about to connect.

THE INTERLUDE

Perhaps it was your love for the things
Of this world that beguiled me,
When you delicately turned in first light
A bronze beetle's lacquered carapace,

Or fingered the carnal whorl of a rose
Climbing the garden trellis, its fleshy
Petals trembling with dew. How often
You'd marvel at a snail negotiating

Bark chips with exquisite twin antennae,
Its pewter track and scrolled shell like
A violin's sorrowings. I little knew then
It was Lorca's *duende* that lit your eyes

Of cerulean blue or the brief time left me
To stand in their radiance. After we parted,
I'd watch beneath my ledge a magnolia leaf
Each new day from the prevailing darkness.

Yet we met a decade later in New Orleans,
Youth's luster still rounding your cheeks,
The chandeliers spilling crystal and nickel
Throughout Le Pavillon's palatial corridors.

We conspired over gin cocktails, no
Bitters, triple olives spit on one toothpick.
Mornings you'd wear my pin-striped shirt
At our room-service breakfast, black coffee

And Belgian waffles wobbling in cascades
Of maple syrup, the trees tapped in April
When the sap rises, the sugary confection
Distilled and stoppered in golden phials.

Quintessential loveliness but seldom cloys
The palate, and come noon we'd stroll
Bourbon Street, listening to a harmonica's
Reedy wheezing, an old bootblack's rag

Snap like .32-caliber shot, his patrons
Enthroned and brass foot-rests locked
Into place. You adored the decorative
Wrought iron balustrades on the Quarter

When it was too early for saxophones
Squiggling blues or clarinets cooling
Down to a few bleak embers at the end
Of evening sets in La Belle Esplanade.

The Riverwalk brought us full circle,
Tugs, tankers, and barges churning
The Mississippi mid-channel, the river
Meandering drunkenly toward the Gulf.

Suddenly we stood once more on the bluff
Above Memphis, our youth summed up,
In the plangent hooting of raptors
Making wing for Mud Island after dusk.

THE OUTCOME

I. Enticements

I still ache for those May mornings after
You slipped the fetters of your first marriage,
When we fueled our own aubades with ruddy-
Skinned pears rouged to fleshly hues scarcely
Connubial; blend in aged blue cheese slabbed on
Salt-gemmed crackers chased by ice-hot Rhine
Wine. We smeared toast with damson preserves,
Its dark plums bruised and ripe to succulence.
Compulsion demanded we stoke our passion,
Those sultry Delta nights when coupling
With you was like wrestling some archangel,
Otherworldly music trembling in every muscle
And sinew. Only in recurring dreams, my love,
Do I reach for your shoulder tattoo that hardly
Existed: did the artist's needle indelibly pinion
The butterfly or will a spasm of light release it?
Victoria's Secret had just come into vogue; I
Conjured Frank Stanford touching death's
Thin underthings to his lips when the moon
Rises like a blood-gorged tick in the Ozarks.
Always an element of the risqué creeps into
My desire to sustain a pure lexical burnish.

II. Settings Forth

There was no air-conditioning in newsrooms
Of the Memphis *Commercial Appeal* when I became
At eighteen an intern in their sports department,
Where I weathered many a six-Coke night during

The summer. My manual keyboard then began
To shift and tick like embers as I forged on toward
The black columns of each morning edition.
My Underwood's margin bell chimed and I strove
To keep every byline in the upper register a decade
Before I followed Interstate 40 scattering its kudzu-
Hung narrows deep into Arkansas. Driving over
The Boston Mountains, I noted mud-chinked cabins
And wind-raked jack-pines along the road leading
Into Fayetteville; I attended workshops conducted
By Heather, Jim, and Miller, my business focused
On dissecting sunbeams with a prism in addition
To things beyond the eye's circumference.
Less humid than the Delta, August in the Ozarks
All the same provided occasion for whisky runs
And clandestine weddings. Cedars' rough bark
Would ooze resin so pungent a whiff burned,
Swollen ambrosial drops capturing bluebottles.

III. Invocation
Here in the settling dusk of my life I long
To rehearse the thousand variations of one
Song. The beautiful but doomed
Landscape hushed with snow in the field
Across from my rented home is pristine
White like a psalter untouched by grackle
Or crow at all points of the compass. Made
To improvise my honor day to day, I yield
To grandiose imaginings, styling myself
Thomas à Becket obliged to put aside his
Chancellor's ring embossed with golden
Triple lions of state and slip on the Arch-

Bishop's purple stone richer than the blood
Of the Plantagenets. I listen for my father
Chiding such grandiose utterance and ask
You to excuse my overreaching
Self-conceit, and bless me with the homely
Tropes somehow true to my predicament.

NIGHTS ON THE DELTA

I. Side A

I can still summon those summer nights
On the Delta, when my antique Underwood's
Basket shift clicked like a fisherman's bait box
Teeming with live crickets. I'd align a sheet
Of rice paper in the platen and roll it into place
Deftly as my mother putting her white pinafores
Through a wringer before pinning a hamperful
To the clothesline. Emerald fireflies were rising
And falling like rootless stars while I composed
At the trestle board table, frosted mug beside me
Brimming golden Schiltz that I lovingly soothed
Into the wee hours during July of my twentieth
Year. You were my motive and cue for passion
Even then; I'd lift cold iron doors of red
And blue mailboxes bolted down curbside, posting
A sheaf of poems meant to evoke the comeliness
Of your speech and its liquid sonorities. A manila
Envelope returned one poem lighter from *Steelhead*,
Edited by Louis Jenkins in Duluth, Minnesota, almost,
It seemed, before the evening's chill dews and damps
Had dried on my palm. Elated, I felt launched in
Earnest, but now I brood over your ledger-stone
In the Murray City Cemetery where granite heaves
At its own glittering mass like the sea. The sexton
Wears on his belt a ring of keys like a woman's hand-
Bones. To him, sadness is a watermelon's heart
Salted down, good whisky poured over the grave
Of a beautiful stranger. Shouldering a spade, he

Wipes sweat from his neck with a kerchief dyed
Midnight blue. He pauses. At his ear, patient
As needlepoint, the gnat's psalm.

II. Side B
October moon ripens colder than a honeydew melon
On the hill's shoulder. Scattered flocks begin to gather,
Grackles playing the raucous bones of autumn. When
Oil tins banged in our storage room my father described
Depression-era migrants, how a hobo in tattered flannel
Would stoke a furnace till dark to buy a side of bacon,
Then fry spattering pork on his blunt-edged shovel.
Meanwhile, my mother's people dined on sumptuous
Steaks or roasts while a bottle of Grand Marnier
Waited on the teak sideboard to be poured over
Dollops of vanilla ice-cream for dessert. The distance
Between their manor house on Greenwood's boulevard
And the shotgun shanty where Dad dwelled as a boy
Seemed wider than Keesler Bridge spanning the Yazoo
River meandering drunkenly south toward Vicksburg.
Now each dawn I part my beige burlap drapes
To sun so abundant it's like slashing a sack of grain.
Genteel poverty has been the wage of lending amplitude
To the protein heat our bodies sowed on satin sheets
So many decades ago. Even now you are with me
In all seasons: when I watch a cedar waxwing chip
At iced rowanberries with its beak or perhaps pause
As a locust splits and crawls out of its larval blister
Into song. I dial up The Beatles' "Long and Winding
Road" on a radio crackling with static and conjure
Those dusk to dawn interludes sleeping side by side,
The spectral celestial choir McCartney deplored

Bearing us to other shores, one banked in the temporal
World, the other in eternity. For me, those vinyl-tracked
Lyrics had more to do with a potter's wheel—"Truth is
Beauty, / beauty, truth"—than some forgotten DJ's
Turntable. Draw the curtain, Teresa.

THE FULL RECKONING

I. Quickenings

A master cabinet-maker augured concentric,
Sweet-scented roses from rosewood, and fitted
Dowel pins into the resin-embalmed boards
Of your hand-carved wardrobe. He shaped
The cabinet doors like ornate seraph wings,
Each opening on the burnished satin gowns
You'd step into with winsome aplomb a few
Years beyond puberty. Then your radiant
Skin would bear only the scar of a smallpox
Vaccination pricked out with a needle before
Seething pustular eruptions were banished
From our midst. Four centuries previous
To our own, the immortal Bard of the Avon
Decried a similar affliction visited on him
By his beguiling "dark mistress."
The nocturnal meetings we shared savored
More of fleshly covenant than assignation
During autumn, 1970, when rain knocked
Russet leaves and skull-capped acorns off
Pin-oak boughs traversing Overton Park.

II. The Southwest Twin

Again I recall how silken-bearded angels glared
Back at me wandering the rows of harvest corn,
A blue-denimed lad agog at ripening maize rooted
In rich Delta soil; I often flailed at circling crows,
Their beaks intent on tallying the yellow abacus
Of each unshucked ear. Sometimes I'd stumble

Onto red-jacketed and brass-gleaming shotgun
Shells ejected by irate farmers minding their own
Crops with lead pellets rather than gravel pecked
From loam. A decade later, we'd fall into
The muffled drumming of a motorcade headed
For the drive-in theater, twin screens flickering
Like heat-lighting along the sky-line. Headlamps
Were dimmed and tickets punched beneath stars
Peppering the cobalt firmament. We'd indulge
In the barbaric splendor of Bacardi-laced Coke
And the opulent fleur-de-lis locked in each kernel
Of popcorn. For you it amounted to a diversion,
You, who'd never once seen a carpenter cancel
His pay with dull lead wetted on his tongue's tip.

III. Murray, Kentucky: 2022
I remember the mist-shrouded October
Evening when I first glimpsed in your laughter
The simple pathos of a moment that rendered
The future irrevocable as the past. But tonight
An ark hoarding your ivory-petaled bones shines
Like a long drawer of exquisite relics. Red roses
Sent to your emerald-sodded plot stand opposite
Your wedded name sand-blasted into granite.
I never enclose a card, not wishing to trespass
On another's sense of propriety. Somehow, I
Could never countenance the notion of being
Loved by anyone but you. Even now I conjure
Oceans of red wheat like the slow roll of a lion's
Shoulder. Turn this page in its own light.

AUTHOR'S NOTE

I would like to thank the following individuals who made the publication of this volume of poems possible. I should begin with Kimberly Verhines, director of the Stephen F. Austin State University Press whose receptiveness to this project and timely advice facilitated the process at every turn. Next, I should commend the unselfish diligence of the following editorial assistants—Mallory LeCroy, Meredith Janning, and Katt Noble—whose efforts on my behalf proved invaluable. I must also acknowledge the editors of the following literary journals—Marcus Tribbett and Janelle Collins of *The Arkansas Review*, Gerald Maa and C. J. Bartunek of *The Georgia Review*, Mark Drew and Lauren Hohle of *The Gettysburg Review*, Ryan Wilson of *Literary Matters*, George Core of *The Sewanee Review*, and Ralph Adamo of *The Xavier Review*. I should also recognize those individuals who endorsed the product of my labors while it still lay in manuscript, in particular Keith Alexander, Sidney Burris, Joseph Candido, William Evans, Cary Holladay, Steve Houlder, Kelsie Jones, Paula Lambert, Al Maginnes, William Page, Rebecca Steve, Michael Waters, and Richard Wooten. Special gratitude is owed to Father Thomas Zahuta of St. Peter the Rock Catholic Church as well as parish members Nelda Allen, Robyn Hiatt, Bernadette and Kenny Luger, and Dr. Richard Schmude. Finally, I would also like to acknowledge the kindness and solicitude of Dr. Bryon McQuirt.

ABOUT THE AUTHOR

FLOYD COLLINS received his baccalaureate degree in English from the University of Memphis. He earned an M.F.A. in Creative Writing and a PhD. in Twentieth Century American and British Literature at the University of Arkansas. Previous publications include *Seamus Heaney: The Crisis of Identity*, *What Harvest: Poems on the Siege and Battle of the Alamo*, and *The Living Artifact*. His poetry has appeared in a number of anthologies, including *Arkansas, Arkansas: Writers and Writings from the Delta to the Ozarks*. He has served on the University of Arkansas's faculty, Quincy University, and Gordon State College. During the 2000-2001 academic year he was Shakespeare Seminar Scholar and Poet-in-Residence at Wabash College. His poetry and critical prose have appeared regularly in *The Arkansas Review*, *The Georgia Review*, *The Gettysburg Review*, *The Kenyon Review*, *Literary Matters*, and *The Sewanee Review*. Collins was awarded the Allen Tate Poetry Prize in 2007. He was born in Charleston, South Carolina and currently resides in Barnesville, Georgia.